I0476977

10 Keys To Succeeding In Business For The Entrepreneur

Published By: AKBG Publishing

A Turning Point Enrichment Company

Gertrude J Chapman

Table Of Contents

Introduction

This book is designed for the new or senior entrepreneur to help you succeed in every aspect of your business.

These 10 simple keys will help to keep your mind focused, choose the right relationships and attract clients to your products and services.

Dedication

I dedicate this book to my Lord and Savior Jesus Christ who makes everything possible. To my dear husband, Alex, my sons, Kevin and Bryan, my daughter-in-law, Jessica and grandchildren Ezekiel, Janixa, Jailin and Chachi.

Stop Struggling And Flow Into Your Purpose. ~Gertrude J Chapman

Chapter 1

Key #1

Eliminate Mind Clutter

Adjust your daily life, by taking inventory of all the activities that you are currently participating. Duties that does not leave any time for you to move forward into what you desire, you find yourself caught between what is relevant and what needs to be eliminated. You may become overwhelmed, or even lose valuable time each day. Cease trying to fulfill duties and obligations that have long expired.

Things change and there is a time and season for everything. Recognizing the end of something is very important. Be aware to carefully detect slight changes, because these are signs of things adjusting. Following routine will cause you to become aggravated and leads to quitting.

Adapt to making a chart and listing all of the things that you are currently doing on a daily, weekly and monthly basis. Take a full sheet of paper and draw a big circle. In the middle of the circle write down your vision. On the line of the circle list everything that you are currently doing.

Discover, if the items listed relate to increasing or decreasing the flow of your vision. Decide to make changes. The main questions that you should ask yourself, "Why am I doing this?" "Is this activity relevant to my vision?" "What growth has this activity brought to my vision?" "Can I delegate this to someone else?" Some things may make you feel guilty, if you stopped doing them. Face the guilt and free yourself from false obligations. Let your conscious be your guide. Always do what is right when it comes to others, but avoid allowing people to control you with unnecessary obligations.

Chapter 2

Key #2

Be Aware Of Your Thought Pattern

Awareness of your thought pattern helps you to frame your day. Believe it or not the way you think has a lot to do with the flow of your daily life. Choose to have a successful day accomplishing all of the things that you plan.

Make an effort to unclutter your mind, before you start your day. You have already written out your plans for the day, so concentrate on good things happening with each assignment. Visualize and expect to have positive flows in every area.

Remember, you as the visionary, sets the pace of your environment. Saturate your surroundings with positive energy and successful accomplishments.

Refrain from speaking the first thing that comes to your mind. Pause and give it some thought, before you proceed. Discipline yourself to be aware of your thoughts and quickly replace the negative with the positive. As you think on things that have a good report and act on them you will begin to see many victories.

Observing victories charges the atmosphere and is contagious. Before long, your team will be energized and believe that whatever effort they set forth will be accomplished.

Your mind and thoughts are very powerful and will attract to you exactly what you occupy your mind to think on. So, think on those things that will lead you to accomplishing your goals toward completion.

Chapter 3

Key #3

Carefully Choose Your Inner Circle

If you desire to succeed, it is important to surround yourself with people who are headed down the road to success. Your inner circle should be people who are motivated to carry out a task at all cost. They see and are excited about discussing ways to reach goals.

Your inner circle consist of people who will give you their honest opinion and are willing to lay out the pros and cons. Recognize those who possess those qualities. This is not saying that you should immediately dismiss your other friends, because you need relationships in business.

Listen carefully and silently analyze the conversations. You will learn a lot and get other viewpoints. Consider the tips that you heard and adjust those keys to make them work for you.

Surround yourself not only with hearers and doers, but finishers, because it will make a great impact in the momentum of your business.

Accountability is necessary to setting guidelines and staying on target. When you want to give up it is nice to know you have others who are willing to help you reach your goals.

Chapter 4

Key #4

Building Relationships

As an entrepreneur, it is essential to build relationships wherever you go. Make an effort to smile and look for opportunities that lead to a conversation. Referrals come from people who remember your friendly smiles and warm conversations.

Go a step further and set up vendor spaces at various venues that pertain to your specific brand. Introduce potential clients to your brand and leave them with something memorable that causes you to stand out from the competition. People are more willing to give you their information, as you give them solutions that will solve their problem.

Keep in mind everyone that you encounter is a potential client, or know someone who is looking for someone like you to solve their problem. Be open and ask for referrals. This is not the time to be shy. Press beyond self and focus on what you are trying to achieve that day.

Building relationships leads to trust. People do business with people that they trust. Make every effort to accomplish what you have promised and give your clients something extra in return. Your clients will remember that act of kindness and feel assured that you will take care of their friends.

Chapter 5

Key #5

Targeted Branding

Being precise about the products and services you are offering will clear up any misrepresentation in the future. People do business with entrepreneurs who have designed a clear plan.

Avoid jumbling too many things under your business name that does not have a clear relationship to each other. Examine if those things listed should be under another web site, or eliminated. Keep in mind what was mentioned about mind clutter and how to eliminate outdated things.

When people visit your web site, what are they seeing? View your web site as a potential client and make any adjustments necessary to illuminate what products and services you are offering.

It is wise to hire a branding expert, since the bulk of your income will come from your products and services. There are certain things that are essential and you should not overlook them. Proper branding is a lifeline to the success of your company.

Chapter 6

Key #6

Teamwork

Teamwork gives the ability of being able to accomplish many things and bringing them to completion in a short amount of time. As people are working in unity it allows for ideas to flow and produces a more effective product or service.

Encourage teamwork among your staff and volunteers, who are taking pride in sharing the best they possess to produce a unique product or service for the company.

Teamwork breathes fresh ideas and concepts toward the longevity of the company. Ideas flow and there is better production, because creativity does not become stale.

When the energy is high success is anticipated through the collaboration of the meeting of the minds. The team looks forward to working on projects, because they are all feeling accomplished.

Chapter 7

Key #7

Quality Selection Of People

Bring on board people who are smarter than you and are experts in their field. Hiring people of such quality, as they work to accomplish their assignments, will help to lighten your load of responsibilities.

Motivated leaders who take pride in making sure that their work is excellent is a proven asset to the operation of a successful company. These people will demand a certain productivity and see it through to the finished project.

Avoid being intimidated by these star personnel leaders. Through their leadership they are capable of propelling the company into other levels of accomplishment.

Be attentive to hire individuals who have a proven track record to success. Learn from them as they have much vital information to deposit into your life. Remember, to journal all the important pivotal points as you encounter them.

Chapter 8

Key #8

Delegating Responsibility

Delegating responsibilities is one of the most important things that you, as an entrepreneur, can do. It relieves added stress and the need that you have to do it all. One of the quickest ways to burnout is trying to accomplish everything alone.

Trust those around you who has the ability to carry out the mundane duties. Allow others the opportunity to show their expertise which gives you room to focus on what is vital.

Avoid projecting an attitude of total control, because it will cause your employees to hold back. Missing out on what a person has to offer is a big disappointment. Believe that those that you have chosen to hire has greatness within them. How would you ever know, if you prevent those talents from coming forth?

Release yourself from additional responsibilities when you have people who are waiting to provide a service. Trust leads to loyalty, so do not hesitate to go the extra step. You may never know what lies inside of someone, until you move beyond your comfort zone.

Chapter 9

Key #9

Be A Solution To A Problem

Focus on being a solution to other people's problems. You are paid according to the types of problems you solve. Our world is filled with all sorts of situations. Scores of people are waiting for someone just like you to solve their problems.

Take inventory of what gifts, talents and abilities that you possess. Build your business, based upon your niche market. List everything that you possess on the inside and carefully design a plan to meet the needs of your niche market.

A major mistake that many people make is their focus is on money and not on the solution to the problem. Money will come when you gain an understanding that you are a problem solver.

In whatever field you will be operating in be the best problem solver that you can be. Sometimes, you may have to go the extra mile, but always remember referrals are gold. Treat everyone with respect and keep in mind that each person is unique.

Chapter 10

Key #10

Community Involvement

Visit community events in your locale introducing yourself to the locals. Make yourself available, if asked to participate in any community activities. Getting your name out there is important. People like convenience and will look you up instead of traveling across town.

There are various charitable events that you and your business may consider sponsoring. Research what needs are in your area. You can either join with other businesses, or host the event yourself.

Giving back to people in the community shows people that you care about their needs. This is a big plus, because it will help them remember who you are and what your business has to offer.

As an entrepreneur, it is a good idea to show your interest in annually hosting at least one event where you advertise and invite the community. This is an excellent opportunity to get the press involved, because they are always looking for stories of good will.

Your vision is important to you, so utilize everything that you have got and take it to the next level. Your vision is unique to you, so discipline yourself and place forth your best effort to make it a success.

About The Author

Executive Producer & Radio Host of Your Turning Point Motivational Mondays on BlogTalk Radio.

Founder/President & CEO of Turning Point Enrichment, Inc.

Author of "Beginners Guide For Entrepreneurs."

Wrote and Self- Published 6 Motivational Books that were distributed to conference attendees.

A regular Contributor to Ezine Articles.

I conduct quarterly Empowerment Webinars.

A Speaker in Empowerment Conferences and Entrepreneur Seminars.

The Author of 3 E-Booklets to supercharge your life.

The Editor and Founder of AKBG Publishing.

A syndicated Broadcast Host on Wellness of Eden Radio Broadcast.

The Author, Narrator and Producer of the Media Training Audio Program "Your Turning Point."

Booking Information

Gertrude J Chapman

Turning Point Enrichment, Inc.

www.turningpointenrichment.com

turningpointenrichment@gmail.com

(407) 668-6828

Social Media

LinkedIn GertrudeChapman

Twitter @gertrudechapman

Facebook /turningpointenrichment

Notes

www.ingramcontent.com/pod-product-compliance
Lightning Source LLC
Chambersburg PA
CBHW070230210526
45168CB00019B/1620